Clean and Dirty

Ming Tan

Illustrations by
Ali Shandi Ramadan

Marshall Cavendish
Children

To the dragon and rabbit, a very special pair.

© 2021 Ming Tan

Published by Marshall Cavendish Children
An imprint of Marshall Cavendish International

A member of the
Times Publishing Group

Other Marshall Cavendish Offices:
Marshall Cavendish Corporation, 800 Westchester Ave, Suite N-641, Rye Brook, NY 10573, USA • Marshall Cavendish International (Thailand) Co Ltd, 253 Asoke, 16th Floor, Sukhumvit 21 Road, Klongtoey Nua, Wattana, Bangkok 10110, Thailand • Marshall Cavendish (Malaysia) Sdn Bhd, Times Subang, Lot 46, Subang Hi-Tech Industrial Park, Batu Tiga, 40000 Shah Alam, Selangor Darul Ehsan, Malaysia

Marshall Cavendish is a registered trademark of Times Publishing Limited

National Library Board, Singapore Cataloguing in Publication Data

Name(s): Tan, Ming. | Ali Shandi Ramadan, illustrator.
Title: Clean and dirty / Ming Tan ; illustrations by Ali Shandi Ramadan.
Description: Singapore : Marshall Cavendish Children, [2021]
Identifier(s): OCN 1244800091 | ISBN 978-981-4974-13-4
Subject(s): LCSH: Hygiene—Juvenile literature. | Outdoor games—Juvenile literature. | Animal behavior—Juvenile literature.
Classification: DDC 613--dc23

Printed in Singapore

I love to get messy,

I like to squish and feel,

Some things need a
poke and a taste —
Just to be sure that
they are real.

This seems to stress the adults out,
"Stop touching and please do not lick!"

Those wipes seem such a waste of time,
When a quick spit also does the trick.

Cats use their tongues to smarten up,
A few long licks and they are done!

Cats spend a quarter of their waking hours licking themselves.
Little spines on their tongues deal easily with knots.

Kangaroos soak
their arms in spit
To stay cool under
the hot sun.

Red kangaroos soak
their forearms in saliva,
which evaporates to
keep them cool.

A dripping nose brings
out the tissues,
When a sleeve would
do me just fine.

A bit of snot is no big deal,
Some fish sleep all
wrapped up in slime.

Reef fishes like parrotfish produce a
sleeping bag of mucus every night, which
protects them from biting parasites.

When I run
and jump in the
playground,
I don't think much
about my clothes.

Those puddles are
there for splashing,

Sand feels good in between the toes.

You can lay down and wave your arms,

To make angels in the sand.

Folks keep brushing the sand off me,
They simply don't understand.

Sand does not make you dirty,
Ask zebras who roll to keep clean.

Zebras like to roll in the dust to
get rid of parasites and dirt.

Chickens enjoy their dust baths too,
Before enjoying a good preen.

Chickens love a good wiggle in the dirt. They shake and flap off the dust before preening: using their beaks to oil their feathers, so that they keep waterproof and warm.

Rolling down hills is great fun!
(Though you may get covered in grass.)

As spiders tumbling down dunes know,
Sometimes you just need to be fast!

Some desert spiders can roll or cartwheel twice as fast
as they can run, a great way to escape from predators!

I love digging with sticks and spades,
You never know what you might find.

I like to bury treasure too,
If I get muddy, never mind!

Yet when I come home all dirty,
With stories and covered with sweat;
No one seems to want my cuddles,
"Go clean up!" is all that I get.

Wash those hands for
20 seconds
Use soap, remember
your thumbs.
Front and back,
between the fingers,
Scrub the nails, get rid
of those crumbs!

Hopping in the bath like a sparrow,
I toss water over my wings.

Sparrows love splashing in the water,
which helps keep their feathers clean.

After I am scrubbed and shampooed,
I save the best for the end.
I shake my hair with all of my might,
Just like my good doggy friends.

Dogs and many animals shake water off to dry their fur quickly, so that they don't get cold.

But wait!
Why is Mum putting
clay on her face,
After stories and
goodnight hugs?

Is my mum a rhinoceros, who bathes in mud to keep off bugs?

Rhinos love to wallow in mud. The mud acts as a shield, protecting against the hot sun and biting insects.

Well I guess there's a time to be dirty, And there's also a time to be clean.

I doze off in fresh pyjamas,
Snuggling down for sweet,
messy dreams.

Five ideas for Messy Fun

1

Find a safe grassy slope and roll down the hill. Challenge your friends!

2

Bring an egg carton on a walk. Collect interesting things inside each carton cup.

3

Mix mud and water, thick or thin. Lay paper on the grass and paint with mud paint.

4

Turn over a large rock. How many bugs can you see?

5

Play in the rain! Splash in puddles and try to catch raindrops on your tongue.

Five ideas for Clean Fun

1
Get a spray bottle. Spray the windows and wipe!

2
Give your toys a nice bubble bath.

3
Shaving cream makes great snow for model cars to drive through.

4
Take a bucket and sponges outside and have a sponge bomb fight!

5
Help strip the beds on laundry day and use the sheets to make a fort before they get washed.

Author's Note

Good hygiene saves lives. Simple habits like handwashing can be critical during a pandemic. UNICEF estimates that regular handwashing with soap can reduce the likelihood of COVID-19 infection by 36%.

But this emphasis on hygiene has led some parents to worry about playing outside at all. Curbed by lockdowns and social distancing, this important aspect of childhood is at risk. Tumbling down hills, getting muddy and digging in the sand are experiential activities that allow us to exercise our bodies and our senses.

Moreover, some activities that we deem messy, like rolling in sand, are used by animals precisely to keep clean. The animal kingdom is full of unique and wonderful ways of grooming to maintain healthy levels of hygiene essential to survival. It turns out that while clean is good, dirty is not always bad.

We hope you'll enjoy this book and try out the play ideas at the end. Getting dirty is sometimes good clean fun!

About the Author

Ming Tan is a Singaporean mother of three children. She loves museums and monuments, heritage walks and nature trails, and has designed travel experiences to reveal the natural world and cultural heritage around us. Seeking to engage as well as inform, she believes that the best stories connect us to the world around us. Clean and Dirty complements Near and Far, which explored social distancing through the lens of how animals maintain closeness without physical contact.

About the Illustrator

Ali Shandi Ramadan lives in Surabaya, Indonesia. His designs and illustrations are inspired by manga, anime and his two beautiful children. Ali holds a Bachelor of Arts in Visual Design from the Institut Teknologi Sepuluh Nopember, plays football and loves running around randomly in the yard.